EPHP

Devoti

Volume 2

THE POWER OF
KNOWLEDGE

Minister Alain Yaovi DAGBA
Divine Source Ministries

Lesson 2

"The Power of knowing God's Word"

By Minister Alain Yaovi M. Dagba

Scripture

John 8: 31, 32

"To the Jews who had believed him, Jesus said, _"If_ you <u>hold to</u> my <u>teaching</u>, you are <u>really my disciples</u>. <u>Then</u> you will <u>know</u> the <u>truth</u>, and the truth will <u>set you free</u>."

Understanding
The Word

It is important that as we read the word of God, we pay attention to key-words.

The understanding of the word is what gives power to the mind and the heart.

The bible says that the kingdom of God is not about talking but about power (1 Corinthians 4: 20)

This power is what we call the anointing. Without understanding, the word of God cannot produce a result in us.

You do not study the word of God simply to quote it religiously.

Quoting the word of God with no understanding is useless. After all, it is the word of God, not yours.

Therefore, by sorting out some key-words (essential

words) in the scriptures, and apprehending the revelation knowledge in them, one comes to know the meaning of the word, which gives the power.

The meaning is the substance of the spiritual understanding. Therefore, without understanding, you do not have the substance of the word in you.

This is ultimately what this Ephphatha book is about:

Giving you a thorough spiritual understanding in order to help you triumph with the word of God.

So let us first look at the underlined following *key-words* in the above scripture and receive the revelation-knowledge within them.

If you follow the same strategy I will teach you here to study God's words, you will not fail to see positive results.

The Strategy

First, you must find the key-words in the teachings of Jesus.

Second, you must have the right definition of each key-word by context.

Third, you must necessary find the conditions and the promises in the teaching.

Fourth, you must fulfill the conditions by holding

onto the ideas within the teaching.

Fifth, you must absolutely incorporate the ideas in your mind and heart as an absolute Truth with the understanding that what is true does not change and can never be changed by outside circumstances.

Sixth, as you hold onto the ideas in mind and heart for a very long time, they will become a consciousness or a personality in you. This personality is the actual personality of Christ or the Truth, which sets man free.

First Key-Words
If you hold onto

Jesus said, *"If you hold onto"*.

To hold onto something is to "not let go", regardless any circumstances.

If you let go, then you have lost grip of it, and you no

longer have contact with it. Take your time to ponder on this.

So Jesus said, "If you hold onto my teaching". The word "If" means there is a condition.

When there is a condition, it means there is a promise that will follow the condition.

In order for you to see the promise, you must first fulfill the condition.

What is the condition? The condition is "If you don't let go of my teaching", regardless of circumstances.

What is a teaching? A teaching is a collection of thoughts or ideas.

The words spoken by Jesus, which are his teachings, are collections of divine thoughts or ideas.

Jesus is laying a condition before you today. He is saying to you, that if you hold onto his ideas that are released into your mind and heart, and you do not let them go, something will happen as a result.

What will happen? He said the first promise is that you will really be his disciple. This means that there are people who are followers of Jesus, but not his disciples.

The difference between a follower and a disciple is that the disciple does not let go of the ideas of his master. He is a faithful student.

The follower could stagger at times, and he/she could drop the ideas of his/her master because of outside circumstances.

Second Key-Words
<u>Really My Disciples</u>

Jesus used the words "really my disciples". The word "<u>really</u>" means there are some who are not <u>really</u>, or meaningfully his disciples.

Once the ideas of the master enter the mind and the heart of his true disciple, nothing could take those ideas out. Even if the outer circumstances are trying to take them out of his mind and heart, the true disciple will not let go of those ideas.

As the disciple maintains this first condition, which is to keep the ideas or thoughts of his master in mind and heart faithfully, the promise will follow. Not only this condition will make you a true disciple, but also *"you will know the truth"*.

Third Key-Words
<u>You will know the Truth</u>

What is the Truth? The Truth is that which is in the mind of God and does not change.

Jesus said if you do not let go of his thoughts and ideas, you would know the Truth.

The substantial meaning of knowing the Truth is that the divine ideas or the spiritual thoughts you have received in your mind and heart through the words of God, must become a living consciousness or a real personality in you.

Please read the precedent statement again and meditate upon them until it makes sense to you.

The substantial meaning of knowing the Truth is that the divine ideas or the spiritual thoughts you have received in your mind and heart through the words of God, must become a living consciousness or a real personality in you.

The Truth you keep is the personality of God formed in you as a consciousness. By keeping the ideas in you for so long, these ideas will become crystalized or fixed in you.

In addition, even if you want to let them go, you cannot. These ideas will possess your mind and heart and will not let you go. Now, God's Mind has gotten hold of you through his words and will not let you go.

Once these spiritual ideas and these divine thoughts in God's words become unchangeable, impossible to remove from your mind and heart, they become your consciousness. This consciousness is what you call the Truth. The Truth is the nature of God formed in you by the ideas from God's Mind.

The consciousness of the Truth in you acts like the personality of God.

This personality of God is called "Christ". This is why Jesus said, *"I am the Truth"*. The ideas of the master in his disciples become the master living in the disciples.

Fourth Key-Words
The Truth sets you free

Jesus added, *"And the Truth shall set you free."*

Why most people are not free even though they hear the word of God?

They are not free because they are not following the steps to enter into this freedom.

Jesus said *"Then you will know the truth"*. The word "Then" means *"only at that moment"*.

Jesus is telling you today that knowing the Truth requires some steps and disciplines.

Jesus is teaching you that the Truth does not set free without you. It is your knowledge of the Truth that sets free. This is how you will come to know the power of knowledge.

Now, what is the meaning of the word "knowledge"?

"Knowledge" means *"to understand totally"*.

However, there are three kinds of knowledge:

- Superficial knowledge

- Emotional knowledge

- True knowledge

First, I will share about superficial knowledge. For example, you may know someone by name and by face. However, this does not mean that you truly know the person. This is superficial knowledge.

In the same way, you may know the address of a scripture and quote it from verse to verse, but this does not mean that you truly know the scripture. This is also superficial knowledge. You know the letter of the word, but you lack the meaning or the spirit of the word.

Second, what is an emotional knowledge? An emotional knowledge is an idea that speaks to you about a situation you are going through.

When this happens, most people say *"amen"*, and they are emotionally stimulated.

This reaction to the words is a sign that they have received a certain sense of hope through the message, but it does not last. It is enough that their situation gets worse and they let go of the words they have heard.

It's like you may know someone's voice and could recognize and feel that voice when the person sings, but it does not mean that you know the person. This is simply and just an emotional knowledge. It does not last.

Third, there is a true knowledge. This true knowledge is more like the ideas have espoused your soul.

This knowledge surpasses the written letters and the emotions. This knowledge makes the divine ideas in the words become part of your soul.

True knowledge is like deeply knowing someone's characters in and out. And in order to have this knowledge, you need to spend time with the person.

In the same way, in order to have true knowledge of the word of God, you need to spend time with the word. This is called meditation. You must see the word as your intimate spouse.

The Bible says Adam *"knew his wife Eva"* and she conceived of Seth. This true knowledge means that your soul becomes spiritually impregnated with the Truth like one will conceive of a child.

When you have this true knowledge, an absolute conception and birth must take place--you give birth to Truth through your perception, your thoughts, your words and actions.

This is so important. Your soul must first conceive the Truth like an embryo. And then, the embryo of the Truth will grow into the full personality of Christ. In this case, you can say that the word has become a person in you. When you speak the word, you are speaking God.

Contently, you will come to give birth to this Truth or Christ in the way you think, the way you feel, the way you speak and the way you act. You will become the fragrance of Christ.

If your words are not honoring the Truth, it is because the Truth is not really in you. Your words will have no power.

You may listen to the word of God and even quote the word, but you cannot carry it out with power unless the word has become a person in you.

If your feelings, actions and thoughts are not honoring the Truth, it is because the Truth is not in you. Why? Because you can only give birth to what is within you.

When the truth begins to manifest through these four doors of your being: the mind, the mouth, the heart, and the actions, you will begin to experience FREEDOM.

You will surely experience ultimate freedom from lies, freedom from anger, freedom from deceit and malice, freedom from depression, and freedom from all kind of unethical and immoral behaviors as well as sicknesses.

Fifth Key-Words
<u>Freedom</u>

What is freedom?

Freedom is the absence of bondage. Anything, I

mean anything that is keeping you away from experiencing happiness is a form of bondage.

Jesus is telling you that all forms of bondages could be removed and broken by the knowledge Truth. And we know Jesus cannot lie.

Now, what was Jesus really teaching in the above verse? I will rewrite John 8: 31, 32 for you based on the revelation we have received. This is what Jesus meant: *"If you refuse to let go of my spiritual ideas, you will become my true and faithful student. Consequently, my ideas will become my person in you, which is the Truth. This Truth will manifest through you and remove all bondages."*

This interpretation above is what you call the spirit of the word or the *Rhema*. The Rhema is the Spirit or the Life in the spoken words. It is what ministers are meant to feed the church.

Paul the apostle said: *"The spirit gives life"*. But you have to know how to use the Spirit of the word to receive Life in you.

Getting the Rhema is one thing. Using the Rhema is another. And I will teach you how to do it.

This is your spiritual practice. The Spirit of the

word is the meaning of the word. It has life.

Jesus said, "My words are spirit and life", which means, "My words have meaning and are filled with divine energy".

Practicing the Rhema

You will *make* the Spirit of the word personal and pray it.

Praying the word is called confession or affirmation.

It is by affirming the Spirit or the Rhema of the word that it enters into your soul to "makes love" to the soul thus give birth to Truth.

You must affirm the Rhema with faith and a lot of emotions and absolute conviction to give it power and speed to work.

Here is the Spirit or the Rhema of the word one more time:

"If you refuse to let go of my spiritual ideas, you will become my true and faithful student.

Consequently, my ideas will become my person in you, which is the Truth. This Truth will manifest through you and remove all bondages."

Now, you must make it personal.

"I refuse to let go of the spiritual ideas of Jesus

Christ, because I am his true disciple. I know the Truth and the Truth manifests itself through my thoughts, words, feelings and actions. I give birth to Christ through the four doors of my being today and forever. I have no bondage in the name of Jesus. Amen"

Advice

Please affirm this Rhema many times until it possesses you. In front of any situation, recall it and it will answer.

Visit Us On

www.dsmchrist.org

Printed in Great Britain
by Amazon